DEAD WITHIN

The Poetries

DILIP MEHTA

ISBN
Paperback 979-8-89699-766-5
Hardcase 979-8-89744-256-0

Contents

We are meant to fall!

While walking through the alley of my memories,
Caught a few glimpses through the windows of moments.
Nostalgic and humorous, it felt...
But despair ran deep within.

Many came and lost all of them, like a tree in autumn.
Some were sweet to remember, some taught me, and a few made me tremble.
Nevertheless, they had one thing in common...
I was never their preference.

Initially in denial, but I made peace with my acceptance.
I am a leaf in an autumn meant to fall.
Regrow and be green, my desired fate I thought;
But no matter what, my fate was to fall.

To fall in the eyes of others, in my own eyes too—
To regrow somewhere else until they discover
I am not the person they ought to be with.
Every time, something felt off in me, I guess.

However, I shall never lose hope.
Spring is at the doorstep, I heard.
After a long time, I shall see myself green again.
Hope kept me alive; spring never returned.

Time passed, and the dance of seasons never stopped.

Winter and autumn turned by turn, came and went.

I never felt warmth... Hope seems scattered;

Vision fading... losing hope and aspirations.

I think I am dying, yet a voice within me still whispers:

The time has not come yet; we might be on the ground,

But we are not losing... we are a leaf...

We fall, we lose our meaning for the tree to have an ounce of ours.

I won… when I was defeated

In the museum of my failed attempts,
The souvenir of my failures decorated.
Each reminds me of my desperation
To be above and successful, I once wished to be.

Each passing day, I wished to be more—
More than before, better than yesterday.
But no matter how much I tried…
I was always incomplete, not enough.

I became a weaver of words, expressing my emotions,
Desperately seeking to be loved and cared for,
To be a word in someone else's poem once.
Kept writing but never received one.

As time passed… I kept failing,
Kept seeking… never found some.
Life kept moving, but I was frozen
With my desire and obsession to be loved.

Time heals, I heard, but for me it only turned out to be worse.
As my longing kept growing, the injury turned into a wound.
Lost meaning and desire to be anything;
Lost myself in the pursuit of the value of myself.

Achieved everything materialistic I wished;

Wanting to be loved remained unfulfilled.

I think love is a myth, and I must overcome its longing.

I desire no love or affection but peace within.

When I was ready to lose everything, I tasted victory.

It is freedom I taste when I had no longing but moments to cherish.

I am living finally after being dead for so long;

I won… when I truly was defeated.

Gloom in the gleam

In the darkness blooms the Cestrum Nocturnum of light;
So does the darkness hiding somewhere in the radiance.
Each aspect of life balanced by the other opposite.
Look around, don't you think the same applies to people?

The gleaming faces might be hiding gloominess.
The laughs and kindness seem suspicious, don't they?
They might be true, but I always doubt.
I think humans might transcend, but the darkness sticks around.

Deep in the core lies the tendency to betray,
To cheat when interest meets their desired way.
Anything and everything is right, till it justifies
The means to their subjectively beneficial soul decay.

Even if peace is served on their platter,
They find a way to discriminate and promote violence.
All their aspirations to feel superior to their own race,
Unleashing wrath to incite fear in those who dare to stand.

Driven by their greed, the insatiable hunger
For power, wealth, and fame.
No matter how much they receive, it's never enough
For their lust to descend and fade.

I failed to nurture a relationship with other humans,

As whenever I see them, I see the shadow lurking.

Even honest interaction—I think it's all manipulation.

What is honesty but an attempt to showcase you are true?

In this fake world, truth means nothing but an illusion to control.

Being altruistic is to call others for one's own exploitation.

Letting the dark side live, the good in you feels protected—

Behold the protector of innocence, the dead and dark within.

The unfortunate

Amongst the green, lush mountains,
There I am lying calmly,
Surrounded by people appreciating me,
Reflecting the sky as it is.

The reality seems quite joyous,
But the truth, if told, sounds like horror.
Everyone around admires me,
But they do so only when I am alive as per their wish.

Once emptied, solitude is my only friend,
No longer their favorite—a forgotten memory to them.
Mortals are interest-driven,
Not even true to their own selves.

Each rain, when I am filled and come out perfect,
Graced by the sky and storm indeed.
Then these mortals return to me—
Once again, admiration I receive.

I have seen ages pass; whom I loved is far apart.
I reflect on her, but she never does.
She completes me when I am just all brown;
I am enough for a while; forever seems a dream to me.

I aspire to meet my ascended self—

Vastness unrestricted, reflecting the whole sky and beyond.

I keep waiting for an opportunity to pass;

The river of fate always takes another turn.

I am purposelessly drifting through time,

With no inherent meaning; never loved unconditionally.

All they seek is to mold perfection in the shape of their thoughts;

Therefore, I am abandoned... I am an unfortunate lake...

The facade

In the good old days, the circus came to my town.
I bought tickets and went in eagerly,
So many acts and gymnastics to experience.
Among them, I discovered a latent fear.

With a cartwheel, enters the Joker,
His painted face hiding the truth,
Striking fear and disturbance in my mind.
The fake, loud laughter sent shivers down my spine.

I laugh whenever I remember it;
Ironically, this world is also a circus.
People wearing masks all day long,
Faking happiness to conceal their boredom.

Who cares?

False relations and shallow interactions,

All trying to escape their false lives,

Riding their unicycle of existence.

Creating hope, though the end is always death.

Why live a life of lies, deceiving oneself?

Why desire fleeting happiness?

Why not remain indifferent, as nothing goes as planned?

Why should I strive if death is inevitable?

I give up; that's the new bravery.

Enough of conforming to norms.

I wish to forge my own path for a while.

I will depart with no regrets, but disassociated.

I will wear the mask of falsehood for the world of façade,

Hiding my true self, appearing flawless,

I am broken, but none shall know.

Who cares? I am a moth drawn to the flame.

Absurd...

Death seems inevitable, a true juggernaut, I guess.
Then why should I run in this fast-paced world,
If the destination is a frosting winter and a slow-paced end?
The enormous gathered, unattended as I left.

Everyone desires possessions, something greater.
I laugh and think, what futile things one wants to gather.
I have my hands empty, nothing even in my mind.
I see this world has nothing for me, nor do I.

So absurd this world is; in its deepest core, I feel.
Still, people see meaning in the meaningless.
The random shape of clouds looks like something to them,
When I see they're just clouds shaped by air.

Am I the only one twisted, I feel?
Or are there others who see reality the way it is?
Why draw water from an empty well? I don't understand.
There are people still able to erase their parched throats.
The brave saw meaning in dying for the greater good.
The wise are depressed as they don't know what to do.
This world is nothing but a circus of fools;
Only a fool sees things that are not at all true.

I do not subscribe to the narrative of society,

Built on the delusion of a few men they think greatly good.

I will carve my own path and walk my own way.

But wait… Life is absurd, so nothing should I do?

I think I'll rest at the mountain peak,

Look down and enjoy the show of ignorant fools.

Reality is twisted and a projection of collectiveness.

However, I don't care whether the world burns or goes cool.

Not enough

As a child, I was complete and full,

Twinkling innocence and tears of purity.

Behold the eyes, home to the rarest of virtues,

The untainted soul, sprouting to be more.

I wished to be great and good, a helper to humankind,

Wanted to serve society and the people around.

Saw the world as a paradise I would love to embrace,

But nothing remains the same as I grew up.

Society discriminates, forces uniformity,

Killing freedom and creativity; if not molded, it's the end.

Be controlled and have a life that is nothing more than formality;

Life is constant, and each moment a death.

I wish to fit in but not be jailed;

I want to be in the crowd but not be a part of it.

I know I am perfection in a mortal body;

It's all a facade to hide the broken self and pain.

This world is dystopia in the guise of beauty;

All minds are controlled and programmed.

I wish for freedom and bliss, not despair,

But truth be told, life is a form of despair.

I've tried and failed many times; to be myself is hard.

No one accepts you as you are until you wear a mask.

Either live the way they desire you to be,

Or you always have the option to be alone and depressed.

No matter how strong you are, you'll succumb to them.

Either meet your end by your own hands,

Or get accepted with a facade on.

I am timid; death is brave... I choose the mask to at least carry on.

The undeserved

Some say it's a fleeting feeling, the butterflies in the stomach.
I've even heard the feeling is enigmatic, known to fade.
It's an unconditional and out-of-this-world emotion.
Once love hits, there's no turning back.

However, I do not know how it feels.
I've never felt that feeling, nor has anyone made me feel it.
Standing all alone on a desolate road,
No one was walking—just me in the cold rain.

Who loves a moth when butterflies flutter around?
Who loves a broken mirror whose reflection is flawed?
Everyone seeks beauty to love, beauty to admire.
Even love has standards, which I suppose I do not meet.

Neither hated nor loved, I am a living undead,
Walking amongst the masses, noticed by none.
I've tried to be perfect to be cared for,
But perhaps failed to fit into their mold.

I cursed myself, hated myself; I never loved myself.
The fault lies in my stars; I am the reason for my own fall.
I am broken, imperfect, and unable to improve.
We receive what we deserve; I am the loose end.

My plate remains empty, my stomach unfilled.

The hollow of my heart desires to cease beating.

My mind is losing its sanity; all I ask for is an ounce of love.

The world may end, but I shall never receive it.

I suppose solitude and disappointment are my friends.

Wherever I go, I am just a stinking mess.

Why would someone ever come close to me?

I have fallen—deformed and an unloving soul, I think.

Lost hope to the hope

In the zoo of my emotions, all tamed,

Not because I fear they might hurt others,

But because they are nearly dead,

Devoid of their freedom, expression, and oppressed.

In the dark, beautiful garden of my heart and mind,

The flowers withered, but thorns pointed straight.

Greenery all around, but blues don't go away;

The thorns are prickly, but that is what keeps the garden safe.

The more I see, the more I hate my vicinity,

With a perpetually growing understanding of mine.

Fear bloomed into love for death, I always wished for—

The untimely liberation after misery is what I deserve.

The graveyard of mine is filled with memories,

Sweet or bitter—painfully buried underneath.

With blood and screams emerging from it,

The truth is that being buried is far better than being burdened.

The gallery of life is glamoured with the painting,

The painter being me, giving form to my feelings.

The painting reflects the painter who understands you, but you'll never understand;

The abandonment, the sorrow, and pain admired by the people who caused it.

What a waste I feel; the person who dreamed big ended up being a poet.

Each word his screams—people read but never heard.

The deafening apathy crushed understanding;

No matter if you get the moon to the ground; in the end, people are disappointing.

Either you turn bleak to the world or silently express yourself,

For the people to admire you when you are dead.

Never accepted me but bullied me passively through their alienation;

I lost hope in hopeful humanity, who cared only for the mindless.

Gave everything to none

Had nothing but still managed to be rich enough to give,
Someone I really admired and always wished to see.
Being around her was always my prayer;
Being hers was something I always desired.

But nothing goes as you think.
Change is the only constant; not only did I see it, I experienced it.
She was as close to me as a passing breeze;
Next moment, she was a star I tried to reach.

The first thought that came to me: maybe I am undeserving.
She is the epitome of perfection; I am incomplete.
Hopelessly romantic and overly optimistic,
I pledged I would be her moon, close to her utterly.

As time passed, I grew to be a man with a mature mind,
But my heart had stunted growth and remained a child.
I knew I would never have her in my life;
However, my heart always pulled otherwise.

Listening to my heart, I kept starving while keeping a meal for her,
Keeping everything precious I deemed to offer her.
My skin peeled while I kept longing for her;
I climbed the sky; the moon and stars are not alone, I saw.

As parched, her presence was relief for me;

Her beauty healed everything I suffered, it seems.

But there were others revolving around her; how could I ever be seen?

I whispered to myself, "Don't lose hope; she is still the same."

Standing in front of her, she refused to recognize me,

Offering her everything; she took all but I was denied.

Kicked and my heart shattered, my mind was right:

I am undesirable, abandoned; no one is mine.

I shall only love and be loved

Like rivers run to the seas,
The lake dreams of being forever filled.
Trees want to sprout more and touch the sun—
All want to have more than they have right now.

Why am I wrong if I want to be more?
What's wrong with being obsessed with the person
To give your all and wish to reciprocate?
Isn't it love to be two bodies and one soul?

I admit, my expectations are too abnormal and high,
To which she is utterly unknown, but never mind.
I'll manage; I just want her to be mine as a whole.
No matter the cost, I am ready to endow.

I know she is not perfect, unlike me, and I wish her to be.
Aren't I humble? I am ready to accept her as she is—
Imperfection standing beside perfection.
How beautiful and poetic it seems.

The gap between reality and my desire is vast;
It can be filled. I'll pull the strings, blood or bootlick—
The events, testaments to my puppeteering.
Eventually, I'll have her just for me.

Isn't it love to drive your partner to the peak,

To mold her into the epitome of what she is?

Like a gardener, I'll pick each thorn from her life and throw,

Till only my lovely rose in my hand I hold.

I fear losing control; however, this won't happen this time.

For my love is my strength, driving me mad for her.

I do not want part of her but her as a whole.

Once I have her, I shall only love and be loved.

Smile while it lasts…

Smile all day long; have laughs as much as you can.
Nothing lasts forever, nor does joy.
Savor the moment, frame by frame…
For the record, it never lasts forever.

Still, why don't we accept mortality?
Why strive for something that causes further pain?
Happiness is a lie; despair is the truth.
The more happiness, the more despair gets fueled.

Look around; smiles hide so much pain.
Laughter is as loud as the agony within.
Chuckles ignore the sadness present.
Stop faking; happiness is a myth you buy.

I acknowledge there are moments of true happiness,
But all that dissolves into the void.
Have you ever met a person eternally happy?
No matter who you are, you die regretting, guilty, and sad.

Why fear hopelessness, despair, and gloom?
In such a dark place, most of your true self and secrets lie.
This world is meaningless and absurd. Why waste life
Chasing fleeting happiness when you know the way out?

Why not find bliss in being a witness rather than a part?

Why not enjoy like a fool hitting a parked car?

Wise and enlightened people accept the depressing truth of the world.

Suffering is eternal; why not live carelessly in the moment?

Why think about others who value you for your usefulness?

Why not be me, living a life I feel content about?

Like a drunkard, wherever he walks, the path is carved.

Rise above, live peacefully, and let death be a beautiful breakout.

Meant to be a sacrifice...

With an open umbrella, walking in the rain,
People scattering around, running for shelter.
Little do they know how beautiful it feels to be drenched.
Pity me... I might catch a cold... Must avoid getting wet.

Each raindrop touching the ground,
Abandoned by the clouds to descend.
Clouds relieved of their burden they were carrying,
As they got lighter and floated higher than ever.

Why does letting go always make you feel good?
Why not hold onto someone strong and bold?
Why am I always abandoned for them to grow?
Why am I a raindrop from which people seek shelter?

As it rains, the surroundings turn shades of blue,
With the sun providing warmth, leaves without a clue.
The pitiful raindrop trying to find its way,
With others trying to fit in and be part of a herd.

Often, it flows into the detestable gutters;
Sometimes stalled on the ground, stomped by people.
A few times it lands in the oceans and rivers,
Rarely becoming a pearl through the oyster's love.

One falls onto the umbrella, slipping on the sleeves of mine,

As I was crying from my own heartbreak.

My tear falls onto the raindrop, merging and seeming as one.

Is the cloud crying too? Does letting go hurt even as they ascend?

Nevertheless, at least they gain something unlike us, lost,

Descending as low as one could get.

I guess we both are meant to be sacrifices for others;

They grow and we fall—detested, used, and discarded.

Loving my new style...

I am a warrior holding a sword; I will not swing at all.

Out of the sheath, the sword demands to taste blood.

I won't; I am a good guy, unfortunately holding a sword.

I am a good guy, strong and brave, fearless after all.

"Man up," they all say, if one is brave enough to take their route.

He is discarded, detested, and mocked as if he has done something wrong.

I know enemies won't be merciful as I am for them.

The tragedy is, even when wronged, I give the benefit of the doubt every time.

It does not bother me; even if I am wronged and killed a thousand times,

I don't care if my death brings joy to others' hollow sadistic crime.

What turned me into getting into this war with trepidation?

Hated by others? Fine. Broken when hated by those who were once mine.

I took the sword to prove myself, to let them know who I am.

However, I'm struggling here; I don't know what to do further.

If I am dead, won't I lose? Won't it prove they were right?

Society makes worse, worst... and then calls it devil's might.

As they approached, I began to swing the sword in disarray;

Blood spilled and many fell; the gore turned into pleasure.

Soon it was over; I went to fight monsters; I returned as one.

This society killed me for me to rise as feared—dark and cold as none.

Introspecting under a tree, innocence seems nothing but a laugh to me.

This brutality and wintery heart I was missing all these years.

Warmth is like honey for the bees to exploit;

Dead inside, walking alive… I am loving my new style.

Even being wrong but powerful, society takes a bow at you.

Did everything right but never enough for others; they mock you.

Don't think about others; they are just toys—stairs to climb further.

Be the player; play with them; they love it, and for it, they stick to you forever.

We shall never die...

Am I the twisted one, or is the world high?
The world I perceive is incorrect and messed,
Or is the reality that the world is flawed?
Nevertheless, why would I care?

The world is already doomed by the people themselves.
Won't it be great to become a catalyst rather than a witness,
To hasten the process and prevent prolonged pain?
Maybe immoral but merciful—behold my rising greatness.

Bring forth the end as soon as possible,
To create a new world, devoid of the previous flaws—plausible.
A world that would be a utopian dystopia,
Fallen but ready to rise once again.

I wished for doomsday; it was what they deserved.
I tried blending in but was always thrown away,
Discarded as if I were a fly fallen in their luxurious tea.
I changed for them, but is it a sin to live as my true self?

Stomped, cursed, belittled, beaten, and brought to my scratched knees,
I lost everything to a point where having something seemed a curse to me.
I pledged that day I would change this world,
Rebuilt in a way that mirrors me.

Fate locked, but I accept

Once and might for the last time, I fall not to rise,
To be a servant and king in someone's eyes.
Tried hard to be more than the thought in her mind;
Failed, saw myself turning from a diamond to coal in a pressurized mine.

The time we spent together bound me to her forever.
The zenith mind fought hard, but the heart lost.
As if the lotus petrified, but the roots kept her alive—
Undead or alive, is there a difference thereby?

The world was colorful while she stood by my side,
But now what's left is the blue in my life.
The warmth that made me feel secure
Scares my soul and chills my spine.

Holding hands, we walked uncountable miles;
Hugging each other felt like two worlds colliding.
Kisses were more than touch; a feeling of having someone whole—
But one day I woke up with reality turned into dreams.

I knew she wouldn't stop, but still tried to make her.
Already on my knees, her 'No' delivered the last blow.
I was cursed then and there to endure her absence,
While cherishing the presence of love we shared.

Trying to stop her turned into a desperate attempt to be wrong—

To be wrong that I knew was the truth: no one is mine.

Betrayal and interest are the true nature of humankind;

Yet again I lost not just her but also social-life trust.

Warm touch, detested; coldness I prefer—all dead inside.

Coping up, and I won; still cursed but living as I am forever lost.

With illusion faded, I see wisdom shine brighter than revealed truth.

I am always alone, fate locked, but I accept.

Hopeless hope

In the brightest and hopeless night,
In the darkest corner, I found my abandoned hope shining.
Hesitant to attend the luciferous virtue there,
I fear the weakness it brings with itself.

Well aware that we are mortal,
Wishes do not have an end, we declare.
Still, we try to turn 'one day' into 'one day.'
Isn't it the hope we are sold every day?

What to desire and what to strive for, we do not know,
Until we are shown the things to live and to die for.
The pity is, the unreal got real and the truth disowned—
Abandoned and secluded as it cracked the lie we withhold.

We hope to be better every day, to be someone someday;
In the endless night, we hope for the dawn to break in—
To just keep hoping for something better than the present.
Hope is idealism blurring the line between realism and desired aspiration.

Hope is a tool, not a core virtue to have,
For us to be bound in the true mirage.
Like a carrot in front of a donkey, making it think it got there,
The hope sold to us is likewise; we struggle but never get there.

No matter how hard you try,

There is always space for something else.

That's hope for you—the carrot to control you,

Drive you and lead you the way they want.

Life turns complex and simplicity a mock;

Humbleness a disease and little narcissism a confidence to have.

Virtues and vices, no difference—

To hope righteousness exists is the idea of a fool.

Abandon hope and see through the mirage;

The world is doomed and life cursed—witness it and learn.

Live life as though there is no tomorrow; we are mortal!

Next second moment is unpredictable, and we hope for eternity.

Keep walking...

I am a tree losing leaves in spring,

A lake on a distant island surrounded by sea.

I am a cloud lost and wandering alone,

A traveler lost and going nowhere.

Look at the sky; the lightning hit my head,

Falling into the valley to the abyss.

Even the vulture disgusts my flesh;

Life was tough, but even death left.

Fine for me, as I am familiar with it—

Born under the open sky with no one around.

Walked on the earth as if I am a guest;

Where should I stay? Everything seems alien to me.

No one accepts me but expects many things,

Like a flower spreading fragrance—

Plucked when withered and of no use to them.

Strange little blue world where warmth is a luxury for me.

As the tree falls on the roads I walked,

Grass crushed under my footsteps.

The sky tore, and I got drenched;

Even my tears slide and went into the mud.

I saw a desolate rock fixed near the river;

Took support and slept for a while there.

The eyes closed, but the thunder roared—

Even the bear has a hibernation, but I can't.

Keep walking, I told myself;

I shouldn't pause; fate won't tolerate.

I am a lost traveler; traveling is my purpose—

Purposelessly walking to the inevitable death.

Echo of silence

Gave a bowl of soup to my friend;
"Drank but still hungry," he said.
With an empty pocket, I credited some more.
With a full stomach, leaving me, he went home.

I walked on the desolated street,
With the dogs barking and staring at me.
Frightened and sad, I was walking insecure,
Still bought sweets for my family, brick and home.

They ate and they complained:
"Sweets are not sweet; can't you bring a better one?
These are cheap and still to be billed."
Who cares? For them, they just expect.

Truth to accept: loved while I provide, unloved once failed.
Knowing this, why am I still with them?
Isn't there anyone out there? I tried remembering,
Tried to count; unlifted all fingers I found.

They all love me, or are they just bound to me?
I don't know; should I test?
What if they failed and I lost in their defeat?
I would have no one but the breaking silence echoing.

Hardly appreciated but expected sacrifices except for my own.

Blood turned to water, flesh to skin, bone to ashes.

Still, there is always something for me to give;

Took everything but still they sit unfulfilled.

Why do I still love them even though I'm conditionally welcomed?

Being there unconditionally for them— isn't it my weakness?

Exploited every bit, from tears to pyre;

Expected to take care of the cost of my own funeral.

Silent seabed…

In the noisy crowd, I found my silent paradise,
Sitting alone even though there are peers around.
With the earphones on, finding a song to vibe,
With naught to hear, silence was the melody I got.

Cut from reality, the imagination seems home,
A house of brick, nothing but a bickering cage.
Loneliness seems familiar, but the people I know strange;
Even though many tried helping, I need my own space.

I kept running from everything I saw or knew;
Unknowingly I found I stood against my own self.
All the reasons to be happy turned into a wound—
A wound I felt happy while nourishing.

The feel of being drowned and falling
Into the abyss of the unknown, yet soothing.
It is so relaxing; I never felt I should be swimming.
Losing consciousness was a solution to my desperate calling.

As I sank deep within my own realm,
The outworld was a mirage in the tormenting desert.
I searched everywhere for a drop of peace.
I found it when in the dunes I failed and was losingly buried.

The cheering and forcible involvement pricks.

Even though I love thorns, blooming roses make me sick.

I just need to stop the spinning of my head,

Revolving around the thing I wish to forget.

The world, the people, and God are dead.

What's left is just me, the unintentional mess.

Even the devil pities me for the person I have become.

It's fine until I lie lifelessly on the calm and desolate trench's seabed.

Painful bliss...

Being wronged and weak at the same time,
Clenched fist, tightened muscles but undermined.
The heart's wrenched and the brain wants flight;
The conscious me desires to fight.

Pledged to reciprocate what I suffered,
To bring a few knees to the ground.
I would stand tall when their fate swings by their neck—
The end I desired for them, but it must be served later, I guess.

With raging eyes and tears sliding down,
Each drop shall incur interest 100 times.
Their words and deeds will be fully repaid,
As a prelude to hell on my dime.

As time proceeds, So does their doom,
No law will hear their lies.
Rules shall be mine and the power too;
I am the Norns to their sealed fate with a knot tied.

As my words come true with the fall of each night,
The murmuring of the world witnesses the plight.
I won't forget, nor will I forgive;
The wrong done will be corrected with an immorally right.

I might be misunderstood while for some I am benign.

It's fine; I fear to be understood rather than taken otherwise.

My path is one of destruction for them as well as for me—

I turned what I wished and prayed to defeat.

The vengeance for them turned me into them;

Now I hate myself after they are gone.

The bliss and pain that come with it—

The story of revenge that no one should ever be in.

Amputated spirit

I want someone to cage me, yet I desire freedom to be myself.
I want to believe in God, but seeing myself— is it even there?
I want to be important, but I wish I didn't care.
Wish to be somewhere, yet I found myself standing nowhere.

This whole life I lived feels like I have been dead;
The people around, the things and emotions—all a hoax.
Who am I? Where must I be? What must I do?
Questions without answers, and no one cares to tell.

I begged for love and attention I seek,
Ignored each time, pushed to the boundaries within me.
My words were barely valued, so too my presence.
I was born to be there, not an important part of it.

Loneliness befriends me, yet I yearn for true connection.
The devil invites me while I see the heavens.
The throne of hell is empty for me, waiting for alms from above.
Patience backfired; I lost everything I desired and had.

Am I a monster or a victim of my own deeds?
I see order in chaos, yet I fail to order the chaos within.
Each day I lose some part of being me.
The reflection and shadow betrayed me, as they were disgusted
by me.

With the abyss in my heart and the mind filled with void,
Where my soul wishes to drown, the body tired and intellect slumbered,
Here are my words, crafted from the un-flowed tears.
Losing everything is what it takes to be a poet?

I possess dead emotions, with a lease on the graveyard stone.
Who am I controlling, or am I controlled by the night?
Nothing makes sense; everything is an illusion to my eyes.
I cannot distinguish what is true and what is a lie.
My hands are fading; poems cannot contain my life.
My existence is far beyond people's understanding… sigh.
I'm losing my senses, feeling, heart, and mind.
What's left in this body is an amputated soul left to die.

To be free is to be caged

I see the open sky, escape from the suffering,
The golden healing light high above, the end of the cave.
The peace, the heavenly help I wished,
The answers to all my despair are in front of me.

Yet my wings disobey to flap and my legs freeze;
My eyes want to ignore and my mind detests that.
Still, I choose not to bathe in the rain of freedom.
To be free is to be caged—the liberating bondage I suffer.

Am I starting to love the pain I am accustomed to?
The sense of belittlement, the form of attention I crave.
The curse for me has turned into a boon, as someone knows I am there.
Everything that was wrong seemed comforting as I became the center of it.

Is this how it feels to be ignored and unloved for a long time?
The hurting becomes familiar, and love itself an enemy.
The feeling of being crushed, abused, and thrown
Becomes the medium in which I lick someone's affection for me.

If this is the truth, then I accept it with a whole dried heart.

The undead mind does not want to rationalize it.

It's fine to be beaten by the world to black and blue.

Maybe this is the world's way to say "I love you."

I am like a caged bird; if free, there's the open sky and me.

What would I do with the open sky if there is no one around?

The cage is nice even though it is surrounded by fire.

It's hot for a bird like me, but this heat feels like warmth.

Freedom is something I might not be deserving of.

This might be a lie, but told to myself enough to be true.

Holding my neck, someone wants me to be dead,

Yet raging eyes seem more merciful than life.

The constant repetition that everything is well

Made me survive the falling stars of my fate.

Even though doomsday, yet the blazing sky looks so great.

What a peaceful end with a loud noise; the caged bird died
with no consent.

The foe I live

Life tests me to the extreme, and why, I do not know.

I want peace and tranquility, but it gives me a thousand reasons for tears.

If I let the river flow through my eyes, it never gives a reason for joy.

Life is merciless, never countering my wish for death with the beauty of life.

Why am I the only one shining with love? I try hard to be radiant enough,

But my feelings are always reflected, not reciprocated.

I am whole; so, does my love complete—I don't know why.

This wholeness has always been the reason for my hollow trunk.

Life acts more like a foe to me, never allowing anyone to be mine.

In this false world, I tried to be faithful and honest,

But the virtue I carried is an iron ball tied to my leg by life.

No matter how hard I try, I lose to those with the wings of vices.

I prayed to God for help; I kept seeking, but the call went unanswered.

In anger, I approached hell, but the door was closed and never opened.

In the lost world of my thoughts, I find solace and a place to rest.

The only home I might find will be in the arms of cold, merciful death.

I cut myself to die within, letting my soul wither like a flower,

But the ruthless life always sends someone lively to torture me further.

I see no meaning in life anymore, just a journey with no destiny—

Walking for the people I love, for them to be happy and nothing more.

But I know one thing: even if I outlive the people I love,

Life would never let me die. Patience is now my punishment.

For whom I am waiting, I do not know; this absurd wait seems my destiny.

Neither death nor life is for me; I do not know why life loves me so—to never end my waiting.

The bubble amongst others...

The habit of mine to love everyone has brought me to the apocalypse's end.

Burned my value to ash, sold my decency in the brothels.

The people I place on the throne of my heart

Are in the same place I failed to secure.

In the presence of mine amongst the need,

I was not even an option to think.

Unfortunately, even my blood betrayed me;

The promises stabbed me.

When blood wished for my non-existence,

The silence amongst the heart agreed.

Never received love from 'Ours,' and searched but never found it in others—

Who is to blame, others? Or is it me who is not important enough?

It must be my karma punishing me—this life or be it from previous.

Have everything a person wishes for, yet no one to share with.

The numbness of consciousness spread along with the shattered emotions on the floor;

The lively help isn't cleaning it; moreover, the shooter is getting late for a blow.

Clarity attained: neither anyone is mine nor a stranger to me.

Neither does anyone care for my emotions nor the circumstances I am in.

I am dying within, whereas people wait to see the corpse.

Why should I care for anyone now? I am a lost man, dying with each lost step.

Neither anyone is waiting for me nor am I waiting for someone.

Neither love nor hate—love is a joke and wishing to be loved is a myth.

I have the present moment in hand, still hoping for festive trade.

What a fool I am! Pessimistically, a hopeful person

I have become.

There are a lot of things I still wish to share, but words differ otherwise.

Even if I split the sky, people will forget me; I am just a bubble amongst others.

So go away, get busy with your daily chores; live a life that is never yours.

Leave me alone for my Sisyphean climax, as some breath is left but not going to end.

Melancholy choirs I sang all night.

The emotions are so vast, even the ocean feels small.

Unfortunately, the expression fails to grasp.

Tried a millennium of times to let it be a word on paper—

How can a wet paper hold words as I hold them dear to me?

Many people heard my words, but barely someone caught the syllables.

Eventually, the topic changed; my pain became laughter.

With giggles, the despair was patronized; I was a traveler with an empty caravan,

Seeking help from strangers I thought were supposed to be mine.

I left the crowd to walk to the peak with a valley ahead.

The depth warned me, but the trench of my feelings smirked.

I wanted to jump, attain ultimate liberation,

But my fragile heart failed to brave the cowardice.

On my bed I returned, with the song I lied on my back,

Up above the empty roof, the reflection of mine.

Surrounded by walls, the world I truly own,

Until I saw the bricks turning into dust while I dined.

Life forces people on me while I try avoiding them.

Many came as many went; no one stayed—I was a weirdo for them.

Certainly, no one tried to give a moment to know me,

As everyone had someone important always waiting for them.

Honestly, why would someone waste a dime on me?

Even the clown is far better, and I am just a weirdo lying on the street.

The icicles fall around me but never on me; for winter too, I was just a prick.

The Lord said love everyone—I am a weirdo, but that's the fault of my stars, not mine.

It's festive; I am sitting having dinner with the teddies around.

They are toys but far better than the creatures I find around.

They accept me for what I am and never judge for being different,

Singing the melodies and playing rhymes; melancholy choirs I sang all night.

The endless pain

The heart agonized and whimpered to the undying pain,
The mind struggling to stop it while it overthinks.
The soul bears witness to the cruel unfolding scroll,
The scroll that is empty, still painted all black.

The river petrified in the glacier of eyes,
The melody desired, unsung in the caves of the ear.
The words unspoken waiting to be revealed,
The redolent fragrance hanging to fall off.

Why does it have to be the way it is?
Why is there no other way to escape?
Why am I the chosen one people kick astray?
Why is my cry for the mind and heart a fray?

Humans pretend to be empathic, are they?
If yes, then why do they enjoy my suffering in their play?
The people who lifted me up were worse than others;
They lent their hands to fit me in their lease with a smile gay.

The hands hesitate to hold another of its kind,
My legs fear the path I decided to walk as I find.
The thoughts are insecure to the words of others;
Even the crushed grass makes a doomsday noise.

The rainbow does not make me happy and rain brings blue;

The water I drink does not satisfy my thirst, neither does the food.

Sleep resides in the tire's window, but I dare not close,

As I fear the silence or the peace that the closure beholds.

Perhaps the world is not to be blamed for my actions.

How can a lover love if the loved has lost trust?

How can the world treat me with love and care

If I failed to become better and acted undeserved?

White in the black wood

With the beak, I break into the light,
All seemed good till the food came to me in flight.
Everyone around adored and kissed me;
No matter where I was, I was good and having a bite.

As I grew, the feathers began to change color;
Initially, it felt awesome and intriguingly good,
Different from others, more flamboyant and cooler.
Everyone awed until I found life betrayed a fool.

The feathers covered the whole body of mine;
Unrecognizable even as a son of my parents.
I became an odd man out, a reason to be forsaken.
I chirped as loud as I could; only echoes were heard.

With a deserted forest and only my nest on a dried tree,
I feared jumping, anxious if I failed to fly or glide.
However, if I don't, I'll starve as I am already left to die.
Closed my eyes and reiterated to myself: have faith, leap and fly.

With open arms, I embrace death or perhaps life.
Wonders still exist as I took my first flight.
The sky seemed beautiful, but the attacking beaks I faced
Made me question if I was one of them with the wrong feather
or a wrong alibi.

I glided back to the place I was, all white in the black forest.

Disappointedly, I looked down on myself and the ground.

There was black mud; I took a dip for the freedom to fly.

Now I look like them, and so I will be accepted, I anticipate.

The longer I stay with others, the more color I lose.

The facade to be one of them—how long can I hold?

I am a white crow in the black forest, deserted by all.

I bow to truth; so, I lose the desire to be included and understood.

In the corner for my dream

On the stage of reality, amongst the performing memories,
You were different, the dream I always extended hands to.
Rose from my chair in the corner seat of the theater,
While you looked at everyone, I was hardly noticed even by the acting props.

You were the charm of the play, the dance of the melodies they play.
Perhaps, I am not supposed to dream of impossibility but just witness its unfolding.
Perhaps, I do not belong in the corners but in the rain outside.
No matter where I stand, forgetting you, you are my euphoric dream.

The lights go off, and I must return to sleep, to wake up for another dream.
Remembering you makes me smile while I walk, yet it compels me to scream.
I desire things I can't possess, but here I am, beseeching my own destruction.
I know we won't end together, yet it's worth a shot at the dream I stumbled upon.

The burden of tragedy is better than burning in the fire of regret.

To run behind a running bus—at least not to regret trying even though I missed.

Men are brave, they say; it's true I might suffer while trying to get you.

But the pain and tears on the way towards you are worth more than gems, perhaps.

With the sun setting down and the weekday passing its baton to the end,

Leaving the hands of reality, I came back to you, to my dream.

But dreams do not last, as you were someone's reality already.

The fact broke my heart every time I saw you—a small price to witness the sun upfront.

Still, I stood in the corner of the theater, waiting for someday you might see me—

Neither as an admirer or a lover nor a watcher or man, but as someone in the corner.

Well aware I am not worth even a dime, but still, my eyes wish to be more,

As they have the image of you in a way no one must have seen you.

Some stories end in comedy, some happy, and some are just pure tragedy.

As my love is incomplete but poetically eternal for you,

Mine will be something else—a story of tragicomedy. I loved you,

But in all ways, no matter what, I am always in the center—as the joke is on me.

Shattered self

I woke in the morning with the mirror placed in front,

Shattered and fragmented, the mirror reflected my mutable face.

Amongst the numerous shattered reflections of mine, I stood confused;

Even though I gathered strength, yet I chose the face I always chose.

I knew who I was supposed to be today, built it and upheld it together,

But with each step and smile passed on the busy running street,

I changed a few times; the real became unworthy, and the lie respected.

I am so complicated, it seems; my whole struggle is to define myself simply.

Every moment another imposed; with no choice, I just had to wear it.

The tree grew taller and broader but remained hollow and worthless.

On each branch, a relation of leaves grew but would dry if truth told.

No matter what I do, the illusion is what makes me true.

From my rotting soul, love blossoms and the fragrance flies.

I fall into the void of meaning while questioning the viability of dying.

No one knew the taste of the poison kept on the dining table,

As I gulped it all at once so nobody would know the feeling of being alone.

I am forced to live while I wish to die or at least be left in solitude,

As I have nothing but my own pain and confusion to offer.

As I kept writing all my despair in the diary, the pages finished but ink remained—

Filled with just 'why,' as I ponder my own existence.

The vanity of being strong to endure the suffering;

I wanted to end the despair, but the hands never obeyed me.

Left with no choice but to wait for the inevitable end—

The doomsday, the annihilation; I wish to be preponed.

The untold story echoes in the bones of mine, craving to be told,

Hiding under the mask, eyes aching as the tears implode.

I live in light; I stay in dark; I wish to be real but survive in imagination.

The desire to be accepted, the wish to be loved—all a hoax yet I want.

Abstract

I desired to be safe, built walls to keep dangers out;

Lately realized, I am a prisoner and my desire a cage.

I wanted freedom, where nothing binds my choice anymore—

Abundance overwhelmed, the freedom to choose a freezing golden shackle.

I looked above for the greater hope to shine upon me;

With the height increased, the deeper the grave for bets to lose.

I prayed to be surrounded by people I can blindly trust—

So does the curse of wounds in the future deepen.

I had great aspirations, but the resources failed to meet;

What had more to lose but nothing to gain?

The more I acquired, the less happiness I felt;

Eventually, the acquisition is added to the pile of my losing bets.

All this material doesn't matter to me anymore—

The blanket I throw and standing in the sun for warmth.

Why has such complexity in life become a trend?

I want love and to be loved; that's what will bring a smile during my last breath.

I loved everyone and thought everyone loved me;

In the bouquet of roses, there was hatred pricking like thorns.

No matter how good I try to be, always the opposite gets stronger too—

The more the light, the darker the darkness; and otherwise exists too.

The wintery warmth

When I was a bud, the climate was cold and dry, with a few warm icicles.

The climate never changed, but I did; in the deserted winter, I stood alone as a tree.

With time, the surroundings changed; many plants grew and waned,

But I remained steadfast, hoping for someone who could stay a little longer than they.

The winter began to take its leave as my guardian angels heard my prayer.

My eyes witnessed the vibrant dance of colors other than blue and white:

The orange of warmth, the red of blood, the yellow of life, and the green so familiar.

So happy with so many like me around, I felt a part of a crowd after so long.

Within the crowd, I was alongside people like me, but we were more unlike than alike.

Different lives, experiences, and insights; I was a tree hollowed by the winters.

I was laughed at, patronized for the innocence and weak social skills I had.

I longed for the crowd to be understood, but I was thrown from a valley to a marsh.

The more I stayed alongside someone, the more I wanted to part ways.

I want a crowd, but deep in my dead heart, I long for solitude.

I want to walk alone, talk to myself, and quarrel with God for the life bestowed.

I want to live like the undead, away from everyone, waiting for the sunny end.

When love knocks on my door, the mind goes skeptic, and the heart says, "Impossible, bro!"

We want to be unloved and uncared for, left like garbage on the streets of the unbothered.

Lying in the corner of my room, with no one around and all the amenities of mankind,

On the couch, looking at the sky, wishing for someone to come and say goodbye—for the loneliness to feel.

I am not made for the world, nor is the world made for me;

I am an anomaly suffering silently.

Neither do the divine understand nor the people around.

I do not want to be encased in a mold like the whole world is devised to be.

I want to be free—free from the sickle of life, from the chains of society; I want to be caged in desolation.

Learned foolish

I felt invulnerable in the times of immense sunlight,
An immortal who can savor each second for eternity.
With a smile and good things happening,
The reality was nothing but a dream feeling so real.

But nothing stays as it is for long, not for me particularly.
So, knock on the door—despair standing at my doorstep,
Like a burglar entering my home even though I denied many times.
All the celebration faded like the flame of a candle doused.

The helplessness forced me to feel the mortality I bear.
The fragility of life I was dancing on for so short.
Everything and everyone I had alongside standing
Were not found, no matter where I turned my face.

People are selfish, but I am a great fool for sure.
I know they'll betray; I know they are not mine.
Still, like a clown, I dance and entertain.
They laugh and smile, but they hide how much they detest me.

Till now I should have been habitual to the hate,
But I am not; life seems to care a bit for me.
Like broken glass, it repairs me just to be broken again—
A painting painted over and over again to be blacked later.

Like a river, people enter to wash their sins, but in return, they contaminate it.

Like a fire, they use me to burn their gloom, but I am made to consume shite.

What a life; I want to be good but always end up being exploited.

In happy times, I spread happiness, but in despair, I stand alone.

I learned my lesson; still going to repeat the same.

Being used seems like an instinct; I am supposed to follow.

After all, I am useless—good at nothing but still being used.

A small price to pay to be around people, even if I dislike them.

The reflection of radiant one

In the dark, gloomy infinite void, there is a radiant one lying,
The only source of light, but still like a speck in the night sky.
The golden-tinted one floating in the abyss of his own mind,
A hebetate expression of a gleamy fading knight.

There came a pillory, fetter, and a handcuff.
Oh… the shiny one locked by the black chains of convict.
The chains extended infinitely, fading back into the darkness.
The shine began to dim; the longing for company began within.

From the mind first rose the gods and demons,
His own nature's manifestation of order, chaos, vanity, goodness, and evil.
Now there was more light; however, the darkness never shrank.
The trumpet of war blown: light vs. dark, gods vs. demons.

It wasn't the war of good or evil; everyone played their part true to themselves.
The chained almighty witnessed a new form of entertainment.
Even though still alone, at least he had something to savor.
The smile, the laughter echoed in the void for the first time ever.

This drew the attention of his own creation; enemies came together,

With each holding a spear imbued with a portion of their abstraction.

They pierced the laughing one, bringing him to his knees with flowing tears.

He looked above with helpless eyes and a pitiful crumpled face clear.

He shed tears, filling the void with a thin layer of reflecting fluid,

While he was looking for pity from the gods and demons above.

None replied; compelled by his own regret, he looked down in guilt.

He saw his reflection, with a dimmer shine than he had when no one was nearby.

He touched the reflection, and so did the person on the other side.

The reflecting hand manifested; he was holding his own hand, it seemed.

With both his hands, he pulled his reflection out—exactly opposite of himself.

Confused and perplexed, they sat together; one was freedom and the other, trammeled.

They talked indefinitely, each one narrating what they truly dreamed; the wisdom materialized.

One dreamed of company; the other dreamed of himself. Happiness had two definitions.

The pillory of loneliness, the fetter of longing, the handcuff of dependence began to fade.

The two shiny ones began to dissolve, resurrecting the one golden almighty, happily resting in the void.

The war already lost

Lying on the green grass, with the wind passing by,
The whistle of the sea and the open sky.
Dreaming of the girl I loved and adored,
The breeze reminds me of her touch as if she is nearby.

Her eyes rolling over the place, seeking me
As she always wished for me to be by her side.
Every wish is fulfilled, but the question is,
'How long will a wish last once fulfilled?'

The heaven turned into a ruin of war; it's him I roar—
We holding a sword for each other's throat.
There she stands on the hilltop,
With joined hands, praying for safeguard.

I slay thousands and heap them behind me,
But I can't slay that just one person in front of me.
For his shield being weak but her prayers were his elixir,
The constant wish for my defeat.

With a sigh, I moved towards him; doesn't matter—
Eventually, I will force her to learn to love me.
Blazing eyes and a swift movement of hand,
The sword almost got him but…

She shouted: "You'll have my body!
What is a body without a loving soul for you?
Indeed, what is a body without strength,
A mind without memories, and a heart without love?"

"Go!" I exclaimed; what a waste I have become.
All my efforts for her, nothing but entertainment.
The dead rose laughing at my plight;
What a pity for a living man to be dead all his life.

Should I kill myself? No, that's weak.
Should I live? That feels so burdening.
Meanwhile, a sudden last thank you hug from her
Took away the last speck of hope I preserved.

The talk of Necros

In the midnight, at the graveyard under the moonlight of the new moon,

The dead rose from their graves to exchange some words with me.

Here I summon the rotted bones from the ground so holy—

Hear my question, answer me, guide me, oh… restless teeth.

I wish to be powerful like an elephant; no one dares to confront.

Everything within reach, nothing out of my hands.

What good is power when, in the end, all you have is a gravestone as a mate?

May you have endless control; still, you're powerless to the betrayal of fate.

Then I wish to have infinite wealth that never ends.

With pockets full, I am free while the fates are imprisoned.

What about your own people, ready to have your throat for your wealth?

Money brings comfort, but then all it brings is a curse—fear of losing and restlessness.

I'll handle it with care; simple life while the money multiplies.

Nice thought: enjoy your life with money and make as much as you can.

When dead, the only wealth you have is the dirt and rot with everything lost.

Love, care, earn and spend… there is nothing that you can bring with your death.

What if I pray and please the Almighty one, all-powerful and benevolent lord?

Won't he help me in the afterlife once I am bones and rattles?

Alas! He only watches and never helps; I asked for his mercy; here I am in bane.

He only loves his praises; only one who can help is you; rest are leeches.

What should I do if power and wealth are like erasers for writing on the wall?

Life in itself has no essence; why do you need a purpose or desire to live?

Can't you live for the sake of living until Thanatos greets you in the morning?

Oh… brainless! How can someone survive when he doesn't know why to live?

Man can only survive when he finds something sweeter than the kiss of death.

Laughingly, the bones replied: "Nothing is sweeter than the charm of death; no one returns after all.

Come join us… leave the futility; be the light people worship, be the void away from pain and life."

"No!" I exclaimed… "Give me power and wealth; I summon for the wishes I hold."

In the echoes: "We grant you your wishes; let life be the puppet and you the puppeteer."

Remember my warning: even the immortal loses against the smile of Azrael.

Years later…

Tell me what you wish; I shall grant you everything, but remember:

Life is a golden knife; it kills but steadily while you appreciate its shine.

Want to be stifled....

In the middle of the silent night,

The crackling of the broken, hollow heart,

The distressed scream of a pitiful soul—

Unheard by everyone but me...

In the corner of the insensible room,

Hugging my knees for tenderness.

But the room is cold, and the night unforgiving;

Here I am alone, the lonely morning extrovert.

The wind is icy; the darkness seems soothing.

The hush is so loud, I can hear my thoughts louder.

Each voice blames me for the weakness I display.

To accept weakness is a strength, isn't it? I consoled myself.

From the gaps of the curtain entered the moonlight;

Even in the bleak darkness, there is something that shines.

What if I have the light within me that fills the emptiness?

Searched and introspected—only oblivion with endless depression.

What should I do? How am I supposed to survive when the sun is dead?

The heavens lying, and the sky bullying me with clouds.

The distastefulness of life, the loneliness, and the solitude to which I am bound—

There is no escape nor any solace to find.

The mirror does not reflect my smile;

Neither does the bed feel comfortable.

The couch pricks, and the light is unbearable;

I want to rest and lie down, but Nyx seems to have a hold of me.

I paused and stilled my mind—abyss without-within,

Studying my own life, the maze of Minos to survive.

At least it soothes with a lie: I am not lost—it is a delight.

What if I do not have the light, but I am the light desiring to be stifled at night?

Rotted flowers

In the spring, when the leaves renew and the flowers bloom,
The land turns green and the sky clear, cloudless blue.
Sweaters thrown and light clothes worn,
Here comes life after the cold and unbearable frost.

However, for me, the corner remained; nothing changed.
As destined, I turned blacker with each passing day.
In the glass bottle full of water, there I am trying to stay—
Against nature, but for the will of my man, I am a stick of rose
at life's bay.

I was a gift amongst my siblings in the bouquet;
All were sad then, and I was all fine, joyous and red.
Even though they looked terrible and out of life,
I was the one to be pitied while they accepted their fate.

Out of the bouquet, unfortunately, I was the lucky chosen one—
The bouquet thrown with the cheer of them chained in there.
While I was tendered, kissed, and then placed in the bottle just
in front,
Every morning, they stood before me, reminding me of their
special day they kissed.

Awed I was while looking at them, but life changed when they disagreed.

I was growing old, my petals turning shades of red, losing breath—

A souvenir for them; I was then and there from the front to the corner.

Once loved, now begged; I am supposed to survive no matter what anyway.

Then they separated; I witnessed the quarrel and the throwing of objects.

But I was never thrown; no matter how much I wished, I was safe.

The woman left with a man's tear and a broken heart at home—

I was hugged; tears were supposed to be rejuvenating, but it was poison.

My siblings would have decayed by now with respect;

Here I am starving with brown water and ignored by purpose.

How can I survive more if I am a memory to him which he ignores?

I am rotting, decaying while I try to survive more—

An undead with a speck of soul wishing to live more.

The Failure

In the lies of life, I found purgatory true,

Bedecked with my regrets and guilt,

Glittering with the light of my darkest moment.

The aisle was a reflection of me, which I always avoided.

Life is full of confusion and anxiety;

Even though the pockets were full, they felt torn.

People around waving hands to say hi;

Still, in the bustle, I heard bye, near me, and saw them far away.

Science gave me logic, religion someone to blame for;

My experience ignited the poetry within.

This poetry carved the philosophy of thinking,

But in the end, what was left of me was a failure at death's brink.

The life I lived seemed so worthless and forgetful of time.

There is no legacy; what I lived was just a man filling the crowd.

I lived because death never arrived—a life with a worth of a penny that never abides.

Even death was surprised; whom she wanted to kill was found already dead, defined.

I mutilated my soul, fractured my mind into shards counting to the unknown.

The body was untouched under the guardianship of unbearable pain.

What kept my insanity sane was the personas fighting to emerge as one within.

I am a man of eternal war; without perfection, cannibalizing oneself.

Cracked pillars and floor—everything unrepairable though.

Many came, and I witnessed their damage and hollowness.

Found them happy because I was more damaged when they saw.

They felt better because they floated while sharks ate me in the abyssal sea.

At the edge of everything, I see a montage of my life rolling—

A beauty I failed to admire, a beauty I could have experienced.

Alas... I was unworthy irrespective of life giving a thousand chances.

While the heavens laughed over my prayers, hell's trench was hanging above and over.

Hell was declared far better than me as I ended up being a self-destructive, ungrateful idiot.